PRAISE FOR
THE *NEW* GAME OF SELLING™

"Great book filled with practical advice. Simple and direct ways of selling in today's competitive environment. My gauge for success is if I want people on my team to read the book. In the case of this book, I couldn't wait for my team to dive into it. Great book!

Shep Hyken

Bestselling Author, *The Amazement Revolution*

"Filled with smart strategies not exhausting tactics. Brilliant solutions that save time, increase customer loyalty, and earn greater reward. Axelrod magically transforms complex ideas into simple, actionable strategies. Reading these micro-chapters, I'm struck by how obvious they seem. Things like 'unique service advantage' and the question "why should I buy from you?" are absolutely priceless. Turns out there really is a 'new game' and, since we're all selling a service, product, outcome or vision, these 50 pages could be the most beneficial 50 you'll have read in a very long while.

Gary Goldstein

Producer – *Pretty Woman*

Author – *Conquering Hollywood*

"Brilliant sales concepts made easy. Mitch Axelrod is a true thought leader when it comes to generating profits and closing the sale. Playing The New Game of Selling you create your own fresh, new shift in the way you sell your ideas, products and services. This easy to digest book impacts your bottom-line in powerful ways made so simple you can start implementing "the new game of selling" today and drive profits right now. A single insight from this masterwork will move you beyond selling to new profits, customer acquisition and retention. The NEW Game of Selling is so much easier, more natural and more effective than any other sales game you play. You will be singing a happy song all the way to the bank."

Ken McArthur

Bestselling Author – *Impact: How to Get Noticed, Motivate Millions and Make a Difference in a Noisy World*

"Succinct, powerful sales ideas ready for action. The NEW Game of Selling definitely follows Leonardo da Vinci's axiom, "Simplicity is the ultimate sophistication." Mitch Axelrod successfully condenses the core lessons with key distinctions that you can apply immediately with a unique selling advantage. This book is filled with actionable ideas that will appeal to new sales professionals and seasoned veterans. Axelrod encourages you to take imperfect action that helps your customers get results and see progress. He shows how you become indispensable. You will find the exact questions to ask to open more sales opportunities. Even if you have read 100 sales books, this one will change your game for the better. I highly recommend it."

Sherrie Rose

Author – *The Webinar Way*

"Pure power. How does he do it? Axelrod is consistent. He always brings complex processes to the most simple and easy to implement systems. He did the same thing in his book, The NEW Game of Business. Reading The New Game of Selling caused me a big red rash on my forehead from hitting it and saying, 'Why didn't I think of this?' This book is power packed with solid ideas that can be used today. I am applying them already. Great stuff."

David Corbin

Bestselling Author – *Illuminate* and *Psyched on Service*

"They say there's nothing new under the sun. They're wrong! Selling is an old profession, but Mitch Axelrod brings a fresh new approach that will be welcomed by sales pros and business owners everywhere. It's short, sweet and succinct because he doesn't bore the reader with anecdote after anecdote just to fluff the book up. Instead, it's filled with actionable advice you can read in an afternoon and apply the very next day. You'll be happy you did."

Brad J. Costanzo

Costanzo Marketing Group

"A 'how to' course on conducting business in today's culture. Get clear on who you are looking for. Discover where they are in their buying cycle and meet them where they are. Learn how to make a mutual commitment with them. Give them more than they are expecting now. Ask for ways to serve them in the future. All these tips and more are found this very practical book. It takes someone with great expertise to take a complicated subject and deliver it simply. As a physician turned marketer, this book helped me to get my marketing foundation in place."

Mary Cetan, M.D.

Physician and Marketer

edge. This book shows you why it's about the prospect, and totally takes the pressure off you as the seller. The NEW Game of Selling will take you far."

BCinvesting

Amazon Review

"Wow brevity is the soul of smarts! A new paradigm in selling! Mitch Axelrod completely rerouted my thinking in this short, pithy book, that sells even its own products in the NEW way! I tracked him down for a personal consult and will have my employees read this book. A must read for anyone planning to sell in 2014! Bravo Mitch!"

Marilyn Horowitz

Author and Writing Coach

"Mitch crushes it again! This book is a must if you are in any kind of business at all, whether you consider yourself to be in sales or not. I had the privilege of hearing Mitch speak at a conference and I found one breakthrough after another! This is definitely not the same old tired stuff you hear from one book or speaker to another. Mitch has an amazing ability to cut to the chase and provide solutions that are profound yet elegantly simple. You can build one chapter upon another and reach exponential results if you dare. I had the opportunity to have Mitch as a Mastermind leader for the past several months. I've had reasonable success after 25 years in practice as a CPA, but Mitch has unearthed strategies that will add a zero to my gross AND even more to my net. Thanks, Mitch, for bringing us up to speed with the new rules in the NEW Game of Selling!

Dennis Bridges

CPA and Author – *Breaking the Tax Code*

"There IS a new game of selling. I first learned Mitch's NEW Game seven years ago. I immediately saw how women entrepreneurs who hate sales could play this game. He uses language that is easily understood and that doesn't sound sales-y. Who doesn't want to attract, qualify, convert, keep, multiply and reactivate more customers? When you break it down like that, it takes the negative charge out of it. Mitch has been playing the game for 35 years, and he walks his talk. As Mitch say, 'If ever there were a time for New, it's NOW.' I say get this book and keep it handy. You'll be glad you did."

Michelle Price

Social Media Capitalist and Advisor to Lifestyle Business Owners

"After 40 years in the corporate world as a former Chief Executive, I had all the Old Game habits that were once successful but no longer worked. Once I was exposed to The New Game of Selling and embraced the philosophy and methods, my new career in financial services was propelled to a top producer in just a few years. This book is one huge nugget of wisdom that is well targeted for today's clients. Elegantly simple yet so powerful, I don't see how anyone could not be successful playing the new game. This book is a true winner for anyone that wants to be personally and professionally successful in the business world. Use this book, do the right thing for clients and get paid handsomely. It is that simple!

Steve Apostolides

President, Founder – Retirement Income Advisors

"Best sales info I have seen. I have been in sales and marketing for over 50 years. The NEW Game of Selling gave me an entirely different perspective of the sales process! I mentor startup businesses and I am using this to teach sales! Read it. It will change your business, and your life."

Mark Wolfson

SCORE Mentor and Business Coach

"This book can change your Destiny! It's a life-changing concept for anyone in business. I highly recommend it. I implemented principles and got immediate results. You can change the game on your Destiny with this one. It's short with no fluff and it reads like a mini skirt — short enough to be interesting but long enough to cover the subject matter. Get it."

Mansfield Key III

Author — *26 Principles for a Better Life*

Wendy,
You're a player.
You do change
the game.

THE *NEW* GAME OF SELLING

ATTRACT, CONVERT, AND KEEP MORE
CUSTOMERS—AND MULTIPLY PROFITS

MITCH AXELROD

The NEW Game of Selling

© 2014 Mitch Axelrod. All rights reserved.

ISBN: 978-0-9915807-0-5

The NEW Game Media

3691 Jennifer Street

San Diego, CA 92117

Edited by Amanda Rooker Editing

DEDICATION

Dedicated to YOU, the committed sales professional who plays the game to love and serve.

And to Sandy Swain, for your love of the NEW Game of Selling. We wouldn't be here without you. You devoted yourself to building our Players Club so everyone has a place to play. Your contribution is a true game changer that will impact people around the world for decades to come. BIG Moose!

CONTENTS

A Personal Note
from the Author

"Simplicity is the ultimate sophistication."

Leonardo da Vinci

Thank you for taking your valuable time to read this book. I'm thrilled you've decided to play the *NEW* Game of Selling. I wrote this book for you. I promise this experience will pay off for you in money and so much more.

I am inspired by da Vinci's words. I aim for simplicity in everything I do.

It's harder to simplify than to complicate. The *NEW* Game of Selling is a simple game.

You won't have to learn a new language, memorize complex scripts, or use uncomfortable closing techniques that bring a lump to your throat.

The *NEW* Game is a natural game that fits you like a custom-made coat. Once you put it on, you'll never take it off. You can be wildly successful being yourself.

This book is not about length.

This is a short book, direct and to the point. I wrote it to deliver maximum value in minimum space. You can read this in one sitting, yet come back to it for the rest of your professional career.

Like Michelangelo, I cut away the excess marble to give you the essence. I boiled down 75,000 hours of sales experience to the essential elements. Master these elements, combine them in your own way, and you will elevate your game every day you play.

This book *is* about depth.

This book is dense, filled with the "what, why, and how" to play and win the sales game. It's also modular. You can use any play without having to learn the play before it or after it. If you prefer a linear game, you can follow the playbook in sequence. You control the game.

Most of all, this book is about transportation and transformation.

I'm proud that the *NEW* Game of Selling has created billions of dollars of new revenue for thousands of companies and hundreds of thousands of professionals. This game will transport you to where you want to go, and transform you into who you want to be.

Please reach out to me and let me know how you like this book. Feel free to post a review on Amazon or the *NEW* Game Facebook page. Most of all, I'd love to know how playing the *NEW* Game of Selling elevates your game and transforms your life.

You're a player. You *can* change the game. I'm excited to be with you on the playing field.

Mitch Axelrod
October 31, 2013
35 years psychologically unemployable

INTRODUCTION

I put the phone in the cradle and checked my call log. Five thousand. I hung my head. Five thousand cold calls and not a single sale.

The year was 1978, and I was fresh out of college, selling in the garment center of Manhattan.

The company was Exxon Information Systems, a subdivision of the oil giant—then the number-one company on the Fortune 500 list.

The product was the fax machine. In 1978, nobody knew what a facsimile machine was. The concept was so new that even if you bought one, there was still no one to fax to! I literally had to sell two machines at a time, but nobody even wanted to buy one.

I learned three things in those three months. One, just because you are number one on the Fortune 500 list doesn't mean you can sell anything to anyone. Two, cold calling is just about as old game as it gets. I promised myself I would never make another cold call again as long as I lived. And most importantly, three, I learned that *I had to find a new way to play the game.*

I promised myself that I would do whatever it took to elevate my ability to sell until I found a new way to play the game. And then, I promised that I would share what I learned with others.

Those promises have guided me through 35 years of selling, learning, and teaching.

In 1991, I created and sold thousands of copies of an audio program called *21 Ways to Double Your Sales.*

In 1992, I partnered with MONY, the twelfth-largest insurance company at the time, to produce a training program called *Maximum Sales Effectiveness,* which earned hundreds of millions of dollars for my clients and helped more than 10,000 sales professionals.

In 2005, I compiled the best of what I had learned into a 15-hour intensive training program called *The NEW Game of Selling,* which generated billions of dollars of revenue for my clients, including IBM, AT&T, and MetLife, as well as thousands of start-ups, solo entrepreneurs, and small businesses. To date, I have trained more than 100,000 people on *The NEW Game of Selling* and have had the privilege to speak to millions of people through radio, TV, and the Internet.

What you now hold in your hands is the best of the best of the best. It is the 15 hours of training distilled into a book you can read in about an hour. It is the essence of what I have learned, and my fulfillment to you of that promise I made 35 years ago.

Here is a quick preview of what you will learn:

- Ways you can *attract* people without ever having to make a cold call again

• What to say to *qualify* a person as ready or getting ready in 5 to 10 minutes and know who to spend your time with

• How you *convert* browsers into buyers and transform expensive marketing into profitable sales and income

• A service model you can use to *keep* your customers coming back and *reactivate* past buyers

• Three strategies that *multiply* your ROI, increase customer value, and boost your bottom-line profits

I will be your CEO (Chief Encouragement Officer), and I will teach you how to play and win the NEW Game of Selling. You'll attract, qualify, convert, keep, and multiply more customers NOW.

How to Use This Book to Win the *NEW* Game of Selling

Read this book…then read it again and again.

Highlight words, sentences, and passages. Keep a journal handy to capture your insights, ahas, and breakthroughs. Write down your "imperfect action" steps.

Visit www.thenewgameofselling.com/book for your FREE bonus material. Here is your personal code for this book only to log in and unlock your access: **yR68kUzH.**

• *Free video training for buying* The NEW Game of Selling. Our training has made billions of dollars for our clients. Apply this free training and watch your game change right before your eyes.

• *The "Billion Dollar" Playbook.* Used worldwide by more than 100,000 people, the "Billion Dollar" Playbook contains the most successful plays that win the *NEW* Game of Selling.

• *Supplemental material, live training, and exclusive special offers and discounts.*

Practice daily. Pick one skill or model. Use and practice it every day. After 7 to 21 days, that one thing will turn into something significant.

Join us for a LIVE training. Get in the game today. Sign up for our next live training at www.thenewgameofselling.com/book.

Stay in touch. Let us know how we can help you. E-mail us at help@thenewgameofselling.com.

Are you ready? Great!

Let's play…

WHY NEW—WHY NOW?

Before we get too far, I have a question for you: Why *NEW*?

Perhaps more importantly: Why *now*?

Why are you reading this book right now?

Why not a month from now…a year from now…or five years from now?

Why do you want to play the *NEW* Game?

Why do you want to embrace and integrate the experience and wisdom offered here?

What is your "why?"

People want to know why you do what you do. They want to know what internal passion drives you. They don't need your long life story.

What's *my* why?

I play for the love of the game.

And I'm committed to changing the selling game. If there was ever a time for new, it's now.

The Crisis: Sales Revenue Is Number One

There is a crisis in the marketplace today. In 35 years of business, I've never seen so many small businesses closing so fast. Why?

The number-one reason is a lack of sales revenue. It's the top conversation on everyone's lips.

Everyone is asking me, "How do we boost our sales, generate more revenue, and serve our customers in a way that makes them want to come back for more?"

Selling has never been more important.

To deepen this crisis, people are contracting their spending and being more conservative. They now are buying what they need before they buy what they want. In the past, we bought what we wanted because we had what we needed. Now more and more people are buying what they need first and putting off things they want. You are vying for fewer dollars in a contracting market. Selling is the most essential skill.

Selling: The Essential Skill

Selling is an essential skill to develop to play and win the *NEW* Game. There is so much upside potential in your sales ability. There's a starving marketplace of people longing to be served. The *NEW* Game is not about persuading, manipulating, or convincing people to buy. It's about advising people make good decisions in their best interest. That makes you the trusted voice of choice.

You want to be the *only* person they hear in their head when they are ready to make a decision to buy what you sell.

The Game Is Changing Radically

The game is changing rapidly and radically. You want to be out in front of the change. Old skills won't cut it in the *NEW* Game. Social media and network connections are transforming the game and create the biggest risk for you in business and selling. You adapt, or you become obsolete.

The Risk: "Seller" Becomes Obsolete

Today's seller is at risk and in jeopardy of becoming obsolete. It's estimated that 90 percent of all buying decisions start with an online search. Sellers run the risk of becoming obsolete because they don't get into the game in many cases until the buyer has checked with the other sources and is ready to make a buying decision. Then they turn to advisors they trust to help them buy.

Trust: The Shift to Peers, Peeps, and Yelp

Trust has shifted from the seller to peers, peeps, and Yelp. We place more faith in our fellow buyers than sellers. You and I face a fork in the road right now. We are either going to be indispensable or irrelevant.

You: Indispensable or Irrelevant?

I want to be indispensable. I don't want to be irrelevant. In this book I am sharing my best secrets. I want to show you that I am an indispensable teammate and coach in your success. You don't want to be irrelevant, either. How do you become indispensable in a game where trust has shifted from the seller to the peers?

The Opportunity: Be a "6" in a World of "5s"

Your opportunity is to become a 6 in a world of 5s. This is a metaphor. I'm not promoting mediocrity. Just like you, I want to be the best player I can be. That's why I do, then teach. I become what I teach and get better at what I do. I hone my chops and progress farther down the path to mastery.

You don't have to be an 8, 9, or 10. You don't have to be perfect. You only need to be a 6 in a world of 5s. Be a little bit better—be a head above the other heads and shoulders.

In this book you will discover many ways you can play a little bit better than everybody else. If you apply what you learn, you will become a star player.

I created a mantra for myself. You might have heard it, as it's become a very popular mantra. I created it because I was a perfectionist:

"Imperfect action beats perfect inaction every time."

The key to playing and winning the *NEW* Game is to...

Take imperfect action!

I say over and over to myself, "Take imperfect action. Take imperfect action."

Take imperfect action. Become a 6 in a world of 5s. Be a little better each day and soon you will stand head and shoulders above the rest.

The Cost to Stay the Same

What is the emotional, psychological, and financial cost of staying the same? I know the cost for me. I'm not going to stay the same. I'm adapting to the changing world around me.

Adaptability, flexibility, and bounce back-ability are three essential Success-Abilities™ you must develop to win the *NEW* Game of Selling. The world will not wait for you. The game will not stop so you can catch up. How long will you accept stress, concern, and frustration before you choose something different? Jump in the game, get on the field, and start swinging the bat.

The Payoff to Changing Your Game

What is the payoff to changing your game? The payoff can be marginal, magnificent, and maybe exponential. Nobody really knows. If you stay the same, your skills don't improve. Results don't happen without effort. I invite you and welcome you. I would love to play the game with you. Let's change the game together.

The Downside and the Upside

What is your downside, and what is your upside? The downside is the time you spend to read this book and practice what you learn. You never get time back. Be judicious about how you invest your time. I promise your time reading this book will be well invested. It will change everything about how you sell yourself. It will pay off for the rest of your professional life.

My game is to protect your downside. If you don't feel this book is worth many times its modest price, e-mail help@thenewgameofselling.com and we'll refund your investment.

Your game is to capitalize, monetize, and actualize your upside potential.

You can make one extra sale, or 100 more sales.

You might earn $500, $5,000, or $50,000.

You figure out the upside.

Look at the downside if you stay the same.

Then make a good buying decision.

My job is to help you make a good buying decision by showing you why this is the game I'm playing now. In this book, you'll find both the strategy and the playbook for the *NEW* Game of Selling. I encourage you to play the game.

THE OLD GAME VS. THE *NEW* GAME

I'm often asked the question:

"Can you describe the difference between the old game and the *NEW* Game of Selling?"

The old game was frustrating as a seller and uncomfortable for the buyer. It felt like you were on opposing teams, competing and struggling for turf. Your job was to sell the product. My job was to protect my money from you taking it out of my pocket. The *NEW* Game transforms the old model.

Let's go through the five steps of the game. You'll see how the *NEW* Game makes it much easier for people to buy, for you to be successful, and to have a more profitable business.

Here are five key distinctions between the old game and the *NEW* Game of Selling.

The Old Game

Attract: Ads All About Us

The first step is to attract prospects through advertising and marketing. In the old game, the message was all about us. We used radio, TV, direct mail, postcards, and space ads to talk about our product, service, features, advantages, benefits, and Unique Selling Proposition. We sprayed our message and hoped enough buyers caught the message and responded to it. That moved them into our marketing pipeline and onto the next step.

Qualify: Selling Cycle

The old game was about putting people into your selling cycle. You take them through certain steps, and they have to jump through hoops. There was very little engagement. We qualify them based upon the old "mirror test": Breathe on the mirror. If it fogs, you're a prospect.

Using the mirror test means everybody can be a prospect. But when everyone is your prospect, nobody is really your prospect. In the old game, it's always a good time to sell. Doesn't much matter if it's a good time to buy. After moving them into the selling cycle, next you had to convert them.

Convert: Close

Attracting through marketing is an investment; qualifying is an expense. Both cost money. Making a sale is when we get paid. The old game was all about closing the sale. I remember buying a *24 Ways to Close the Sale* video. It included the "Right Angle Close," the "Ben Franklin Balance Sheet," the "Twist the Arm behind the Back," "Hammer over the Head," and two dozen more closing techniques. You had to learn all these closing statements. Then you had to handle the objections—and close again. It was like a contest, a battle between buyer and seller. Nobody feels comfortable this way, not as a buyer or as a seller.

Nothing creates more stress and tension than the moment when you are "closing" someone to buy. When you did close them, then you had to keep them.

Keep: Renew

The old method of keeping customers revolved around a renewal date, like an anniversary, birthday, or special event. We kept in touch and reconnected with people when there was some trigger date or a product or service renewal. Most businesses didn't have an ongoing process of relationship building and continual engagement. Despite the huge opportunity after the first sale, few companies nurtured customers. It was difficult to keep people from coming in the front door and running out the back door.

Multiply: Repeat

How did we multiply customers in the old game? Typically, we did it through a repeat sale. When you made a sale, you weren't trained to ask them to buy something again right then. You were afraid if you asked them to buy something additional, they might reconsider their existing purchase. You were taught not to compromise an existing sale. Old sales training taught you to go back for a repeat sale after you make the first sale, after the check clears, and after the buyer is in the system.

Here's the major distinction of the old game: it's all about *us*.

Our ads scream how great we are…forcing people into our selling cycle…closing the sale…keeping them when they renew…repeat and repeat over and over…and when we have a new product, we launch a big campaign to resell people.

Tell me: how well is the old game of selling working for you? The relationship breaks down in many different places, which is why selling has such a bad taint to it. When I ask audiences, "Who likes to be sold to?" very few hands go up. When I ask, "Who likes to buy?" every hand goes up.

If you don't like to be sold to, how is that affecting your ability to sell to others?

Maybe it's time to change your game.

The *NEW* Game

Here is how the *NEW* Game of Selling is distinct and different.

Attract: Hungry Fish

We attract hungry fish, people who are searching for what we have and are ready to buy it *now*. Our message from the beginning is all about *them*. Are you interested in me? I doubt it. You are interested in you.

In the *NEW* Game, I send you a message all about you. If you're a hungry fish swimming around looking and searching for an idea, strategy, or solution, I will magnetize and attract you to me. I'm speaking your language, walking in your shoes, sitting in your chair, and seeing through your eyes. I'm connecting with what you're thinking. I'm talking buyer talk, not seller

17

speak. I'm stimulating you to think about possibilities you've never considered.

Qualify: The Buying Cycle

I refer to qualifying a buyer as the Grand Canyon of lost opportunity. After spending a fortune to attract buyers, companies lose a fortune by not aligning with their buying cycle. The old game was about the selling cycle; the *NEW* Game is about the buying cycle. People don't care about your selling cycle. Many don't care about your product or service, issue, or cause.

People care most about getting what they want. In the *NEW* Game, we qualify by aligning with the buying cycle, meeting people where they are and knowing what they want better than anyone else in the game. We move forward together, arm in arm toward the Promised Land. How? We convert browsers to buyers through alignment, agreement, and commitment, not by closing the sale.

Convert: Gain Commitment

Think about the word *close*. It's an ending. It wraps up and completes. The old game was about closing the sale. Smart companies realize the game is not just to make a sale. The purpose of making a sale is to get a customer. A customer commits to exchanging money for your product or service. Customers want to stay in the game with you because they want to be served. They want a result, an improvement, progress, and a good experience working with you. They want your product or service to work. Converting a browser into a buyer is not the end; it's just the beginning of a mutually beneficial and profitable relationship.

Keep: Serve What's Next

When you serve people through mutual commitment, they will often tell you what their next purchase will be. The old game was about waiting for an event, a new product launch, or a renewal date to have a reason to call them. A person can buy again in ten days, ten minutes, even ten seconds. If you serve them and help them get them what they want, they will tell you what they want next. We are in the transportation business. Once we help transport somebody someplace, she may want to go somewhere else next...then somewhere else...then somewhere else. What's next?

Multiply: ROI

The old game was repeat sales. The *NEW* Game is "multiply your ROI." How do you multiply your ROI? You bump, bundle, bargain, borrow, and back-end customers. You stay in touch with customers and continually communicate with them. You ask where they want to go next. Every additional sale increases your profit as much as 300 to 900 percent, even if you've made a big first sale. You multiply your ROI with every new sale, referral, or reactivation of a past customer. The *NEW* Game of Selling shows you how to multiply your ROI:

• Bump: ask what else they might like or recommend the next step at time of commitment

• Bundle: combine a product or service, yours or mine, and give more value for more money

• Bargain: offer a whole lot more for a whole lot less if they add it now

- Borrow: partner and/or joint venture with other businesses whose audiences are your buyers

- Backend: communicate, connect, and offer them new transportation and transformation

The *NEW* Game is a whole different ball game. It's all about them.

You attract the hungry fish, meet them where they are in the buying cycle, gain a mutual commitment to get them what they want, serve them so they tell you what they want next and buy it from you, and multiply your ROI through bump, bundle, bargain, borrow, and backend reengagement.

Embrace these five *NEW* Game distinctions, and you will be a player.

Master them, and you become a *NEW* Game changer.

PEOPLE AND PROBLEMS VS. PRODUCTS AND PROFITS

A major change from old to *NEW* Game is to shift focus from products and profits to people and problems. Old game was about advertising, marketing, and promotion. The "me" message was all about our products and services, issues and causes. We screamed at people.

People don't care so much about our products and profits. They care about themselves and their problems. They want you to care about them and their problems too. Game changers care more about the customer than the sale, people more than profits.

It's hard to put your products and profits aside, but it's in your best interest to do so.

These seven key distinctions will help you shift your focus and change the game.

Serve Them

Serve them instead of marketing you. This may fly in the face of what we hear in the business community. Much of today's business advice centers on how you more effectively market and position yourself.

Yes, we market and promote. You want to be in a position where people see, get, and appreciate your value. If your focus is on marketing you, you're less likely to connect with what's important to your customer and how she wants to be served.

That's why I suggest that the first moment you meet somebody, add real, *not* perceived, value. Real value positions you as the trusted voice of choice. When they're ready to buy, because you've added value and served them, chances are good you'll get a shot to deliver on your promise. Serve them instead of market you.

Align with Their Buying Cycle

Align with their buying cycle, and get out of your selling cycle. I've worked with big corporations, small businesses, and entrepreneurs. I've trained hundreds of thousands of sales professionals from hundreds of companies, including banks, insurance companies, financial services companies, Fortune 500s like IBM and AT&T, and across the spectrum to solo free agents. I ask them all:

"Is there ever a bad time to sell?"

Of course not! Today is a great time to sell. The more important question is:

"Is it a good time to buy?"

In other words, does your selling cycle line up with my buying cycle? Much of the sales training and education I experienced focused on the selling cycle. In the *NEW* Game of Selling, we zero in on the buying cycle and meet a person where she is.

People understand, but really, they don't care that you earn a living on sales or commissions. A buyer doesn't want to align with your selling cycle. Get out of your selling cycle completely and meet your buyer where she is right now.

Shortly you'll discover exactly how to do that. You'll know how to identify the three phases of the buying cycle. By asking the questions we give you, within a few minutes you'll know where that person is in the buying cycle.

It's critically important to identify and segment your prospects into the three phases of the buying cycle. More on that shortly.

Focus on Their Destination

Focus on their destination, not your transportation. In 1978, I started a financial planning business called Money Managers, Inc. We were among the first financial planning firms in New Jersey who charged fees for advice. We also sold life insurance. When people asked me what I did for a living, I didn't say I sold life insurance, because I did much more. A running joke was that the fastest way to clear out a room and get everyone running away from you was to say, "I sell life insurance."

Instead I said, "I'm in the transportation business. I help people get from where they are to where they want to be financially. Where would you like to go?"

That response changed the context and created a whole new and different conversation.

Some people asked, "Do you sell life insurance?" Yes, and life insurance is just one vehicle. What kind of transportation are you looking for?

So here's my question for you:

Are you focused on your transportation, your vehicle that takes people from here to there, or are you talking about their destination, the place they want to go?

Here's how you know:

If you're talking about your product, your service, your issue, your cause, or how you're going to get them from here to there, you're talking about your vehicle and from your side of the table.

If you're talking about where they want to go, when they want to arrive, how they want to travel, and what's it going to look and feel like when they get there, you're in their seat and on their side of the table. You're talking destination.

People are more interested in talking about where they want to go. Focus on their destination.

Put USA First

Put USA before USP. You've probably heard of the term USP: it stands for *Unique Selling Proposition*. USP has been around for decades. It's the way you language your unique advantage that distinguishes your product or service from everybody else.

Your USP conveys your most attractive and compelling value to the people looking for it. Almost always the USP comes from you, the seller. You create it. You may get input from people in your company. You may ask your peers or industry colleagues.

Rarely do I meet a company that develops a USP with customer input. Usually they lock themselves in a room and come up with what they think are their Unique Selling Propositions. They whittle them down, say it their way, and then fire it out to the marketplace. They don't know if people are hearing, getting, and resonating with the uniqueness of that selling proposition, or if it's missing the mark and going right past them. They don't know because they don't ask.

So what's a USA? Your *Unique Service Advantage*.

Your USA is what your customers tell you about how your service advantage is different and unique.

You can't go into a room with your team and figure it out. There's only one way to find out your USA. You have to ask your customers the one most important question of service:

"Why do you buy from me (us)?"

Maybe one in a hundred businesses asks their customers this question. This question has created tens of millions of dollars of new revenue for our clients who asked the question and incorporated the answers into their USA.

When you ask your customers why they buy from you, you understand in their language what your Unique Service Advantage really is. When you get clear about your USA, you can use four powerful words whenever you meet somebody new.

When a person asks, "Why should I buy from you?"

You can start your reply with these four powerful words:

"Our customers tell us…"

What do your customers tell you? They'll tell you what your Unique Service Advantage is when you ask them why they buy. You don't create your USA; you get it from your customers. Once you discover your USA, you can language it, improve it, hone it, and merge it with your USP. Your Unique Service Advantage can be the first thing you talk to people about, because what your customers are telling you is what new buyers want to hear.

Demonstrate Your Product or Service

Demonstrate, don't just present. In sales books, courses, and training, there's an entire section devoted to presenting your product or service. In *The NEW Game of Selling* we show you how to present your product or service in a way that most ideally meets a person's buying criteria. However, here's the question:

Are buyers really interested in a presentation—or are they more interested in a demonstration?

Rather than the pitch of the presentation, they want an experience of the demonstration. This distinction makes a big difference in the context of the relationship and context of the conversation.

How can you demonstrate your product, service, or solution in action? You share success stories, a real experience or a free taste. You're not just presenting what might be. You demonstrate what actually is. In this book we're not just teaching you how to fish.

We're giving you the fish!

In 2003, I spoke at the Internet Marketing Super Conference and asked the audience, "Who would like to learn how to fish?" Quite a few hands went up.

Then I asked, "Who would like me to just give you the fish?"

Every hand went up. You may have heard my "give them the fish" phrase. People everywhere started using different versions of "Don't teach a man to fish—give him the fish."

People don't just want to be taught how to fish.

They want the fish. Slice it, dice it, and serve it to them *their* way.

Presenting is important, but demonstrating is crucial. Instead of presenting as a theoretical exercise, how can you better demonstrate your expertise and show your solution in action?

Gain Commitment

Gain commitment; don't close a sale. In Play 3 you'll discover "three magic words" that transform your business and selling. You'll see why these three magic words actually have the power to change every aspect of your life. One of the three magic words is *commitment*.

The old game of selling was all about closing the sale. How does "closing the sale" feel to you? What psychological impact does "closing" have on a buyer? Close means the end, not the beginning. When a person buys, it's the beginning of his user experience, the beginning of what you want to be an ongoing relationship.

The notion of closing a sale puts brackets around the relationship. This part of the sales process creates stress, tension, distress, and anxiety for you, me and the people we serve. Everything changes when you gain commitment rather than close a sale. It's commencement, a start, a new beginning.

How comfortable are you with closing the sale? "Your pen or mine?"

Does your buyer really want you to use the "Right Angle Close," "Reverse Option," or "Ben Franklin Balance Sheet?" Trying to remember how to close is enough to make you crazy.

There are only two ways to gain commitment and move to commencement.

1.   You make a statement: "Here's the next step for us to take in the process." If they agree, you move on.

2.   You ask another question: "Are you committed and ready to get started right now? Should we take the next step?"

Don't memorize 24 ways to close the sale. Commitment is the game.

Commitment is a buyers' word. It makes them responsible for their choice. It recognizes and acknowledges you're making a mutual commitment to work together to achieve the outcome the buyer wants from your product or service.

Don't close the sale. Start gaining commitment.

Transform Rotten into RIPE

I don't have to explain rotten. You've had rotten business deals and relationships in life. You know how much rotten costs in lost time, energy, and money. A rotten crop yields no harvest.

For the best bounty, transform rotten into RIPE.

- R = Results transport you from where you are to where you want to be.

- I = Improvement transforms you from who you are to who you want to be.

- P = Progress transcends you from where you were to where you are.

- E = Experience transmutes you from who you were to who you are.

There's a massive movement toward membership websites and subscription learning platforms, like our Players Club. On average, a member stays for three months. Here's why.

Too much content! You are already information overloaded. Can you really absorb more content? It's not about more content or information. It's about helping people get RIPE:

- Get Results

- Show Improvement

- Make Progress

- Create an Experience

Help them feel so good about you they can't wait for the next opportunity to engage.

In 1996, Liza gave me best compliment I ever got. When I asked her why she came back to my seminar again for the second time in three days, her five words changed my business and life:

"I want more of you!"

When you help people get RIPE with results, improvement, progress, and experience, they want more of you. You'll never lose them.

You don't have to provide more content. You don't have to have the best product or service. Keep people RIPE and they'll never get rotten on you. Help them get results, show improvement and make progress. Then create an experience they want more of, and you'll keep people coming back and bringing their friends.

The strategy of the *NEW* Game is to shift the conversation from products and profits to people and problems. That's how you attract, qualify, convert, keep, and multiply more customers.

Now it's time to open up the playbook and show you how these five plays help you win the *NEW* Game of Selling.

PLAY 1: ATTRACT "HUNGRY FISH" WITH TUNING FORK MARKETING

First, you need to attract your customers. There are four critical questions to ask. When you answer these questions, you become attraction in action. I call this "tuning fork marketing." When you strike a tuning fork, it resonates or vibrates at a certain pitch.

Anything within that range of the pitch is picked up by that vibration. Anything outside the range of that pitch doesn't know the tuning fork exists. Tuning fork marketing is like radio marketing. You dial into a radio station your customers are already listening to.

It's much more difficult to create a brand-new broadcast station, put your message out there, and hope somebody hears it. This old-game approach to attracting buyers is losing its effectiveness.

Here are the four questions you want to ask to become attraction in action:

Who Are You Best Suited to Serve?

The number-one question of marketing is, "Who are you best suited to serve?"

Not everybody. Not anybody. Not the whole world. Who are you really *best* suited to serve?

If you've been in business for a while, you can get this answer by taking a demographic and psychographic look at your customer base. You can see what they have in common, that common thread that runs through the fabric of who you're best suited to serve. That doesn't mean you can't or won't attract other people. You can. The highest payoff comes from focusing on who you are best suited to serve. I am best suited to serve committed professionals who want to change the game and be the best in their field.

Start to define and clarify who you're best suited to serve.

Where Are They?

This is a big missing piece in many marketing plans. I've done thousands of consultations and developed hundreds of marketing strategies. Rarely do marketing plans ask and answer the question: where are the people we are looking for?

You can reach them if you know where they are, where they congregate, and with whom they affiliate and associate. Your strategy to reach them will be in alignment with where they are.

If they're at Starbucks and you're sending an e-mail or a message through Twitter, they're not there. Your message and their "where" are incongruent.

If they're on Facebook and LinkedIn, and you're sending direct mail or postcards, they're not paying attention. You have a mismatch.

So where are they? Make a list of all the places they are. Now ask yourself the third question:

What Do They Want and Need?

I meet too many people who tell me nobody is buying their products and services. Rather than adjust, discard, or replace their product and service with something that people want and need, they fall in love with their product and service. This keeps them from seeing another pathway.

Falling in love with your product and service today is a costly and dangerous strategy. What you like, what you love, what you buy, and what you believe actually have little to do with how successful you're going to be. People buy what they buy because they want, need, or like it, not because you love it or sell it.

I'm an advocate of passion. I'm passionate about teaching. I love what I'm doing. Yet if nobody out there wants what I have, no matter how passionate I may be, I'm going to be out of business. The name of the game is to offer a product, service, or solution people want, need, and like.

In the old game, people bought what they wanted because they had what they needed. For most of my career, I taught that trying to sell people what they need was only for commodity products and services. Find out what people want and give it to them.

That game has changed again. Now buyers are not spending money as fluidly on luxury items. Buyers are more discerning and conservative.

More people are buying what they need before buying what they want. This is important to be aware of. If you're not selling what people want or need, you'll frustrate your business and not be as profitable as you can be.

Are you in love with your product or service? To make a living, the key is to attract plenty of other people who are in love with your product or service.

Identify what your buyers want and need.

The fourth question is:

How Are You Going to Reach Your Customers?

You have more mediums of communication at your disposal than ever. You can reach just about anyone through social media, Facebook, Twitter, LinkedIn, Pinterest, and the other social networks. You can find almost anyone on Google®. Most everyone has e-mail, cell phone and text. More and more have tablets.

When I started in business in 1978, I had the phone, mail, and face-to-face as my only choices to meet with people. Now you have the Internet, Skype, webinars, teleconferencing, and a host of other media to attract people to you.

The Internet changed the playing field. It fundamentally and radically changed the game. Yet you don't have to rely completely on the Internet.

The telephone has re-emerged as a critically important and effective piece of equipment. At a Speakers and Authors Networking Group (SANG) meeting, Tony Hsieh, the CEO of Zappos, said,

"The telephone is the best branding tool ever devised."

I teach a training called Telephone Mastery. It's a key part of the *NEW* Game of Selling. There's a whole new game of telemarketing, telesales, and teleservice. The telephone is a valuable tool to leverage. Telephone mastery is also one of the least developed skills being taught. Master the phone.

Here are three key components to reach people:

1. Impact

2. Medium

3. Frequency

Impact: Hit them with your best shot right up front. Don't wait, and don't hold back. If you don't make an impact and get their attention, the game is over before it starts.

What can you say, what can you do, what can you send, and what can you give that has the greatest impact?

Don't be afraid of giving away your best secrets. I'm giving my best to you in this book. I'm not holding back. Sharing my best with you about how to be a sales master demonstrates I know what I'm talking about. If I don't impact you with something good, you'll check out, tune out, and exit quickly. Hit people with your best shot up front. Then continue to impact them in every interaction.

Medium: One of the most important distinctions I started teaching salespeople was to ask buyers a question. This question is now common, but when I introduced it in the 1980s, it was a game-changing question:

"How do you prefer to get your information?"

Do you want your education in written form, do you like to hear it, or do you prefer to watch it? Do you like to see it drawn it on a flipchart? Do you want me to bring it to you face to face, or is it better that we speak over the phone? How do you like to get your education?

This question enables us to deliver the right kind of information in the medium our buyer likes best. In the past, we had to produce an audio, video and written document to deliver a message. Digital technology has reduced the cost of delivering information to virtually free.

If you send me a video, I won't watch it right away. Takes too much time. I rarely watch my own videos. I'm a reader. If you want my attention, send me a short summary document I can read in a few minutes, because that's my preferred mode. My second choice would be audio. I may be a perfect prospect for you, but if you don't meet my medium preference, it's game over.

How do you prefer to get your education?

Ask everyone how they prefer to get their education. It's never been easier to provide education in multiple media, whether written, audio, video, slides, phone, etc. The more media you can deliver, the more people you can reach.

Frequency: How often should we communicate? Nobody really knows the perfect frequency. Old-game thinking was that you needed 7 to 21 impressions before people will buy something.

This is not true in the *NEW* Game. The better you target and define who you're best suited to serve, the quicker you can find hungry fish. You really don't know how frequently your target audience wants to hear from you. Tom Peters says communicate every day. Dan Kennedy has a 200+ message sequence over 365 days. You can communicate frequently with people if you have something of value to say or share. They will feel more connected to you if you speak their language.

Frequency is a tricky thing. You've got to decide how often your people want to hear from you, as well as how often *you're* capable of communicating. You may not want or be able to communicate at Tom Peters's or Dan Kennedy's frequency. Ask your audience how often they want to hear from you, and start to communicate with them. When in doubt, communicate more frequently so they don't forget about you.

So, the best way to reach people is to determine:

• How can you impact them most powerfully up front?

• How do they want to get their education?

• What frequency will you communicate?

Two More Attraction Tips

Rejection Proof Networking™

We did a UStream broadcast on Rejection Proof Networking™ and recorded it. We showed our guests how to eliminate rejection and talk to anyone, anywhere, anytime about anything.

We had an astounding response to that program. People are still buzzing about it and contacting us. If you do any kind of networking or offline marketing, Rejection Proof Networking™ is the most effective way to tell people what you do, why you do it, and who you're looking for.

Being Rejection Proof changes everything about how you market, sell, network, promote, and advertise. You can use it face to face, on the phone, in direct mail, through seminars, or whatever attraction medium you use. (You can be Rejection Proof; start at www.thenewgameofselling.com/book.)

Magnetic Keyword Analysis

Here's an online recommendation that also changes the attraction game. You can put yourself in the path of people who are searching for what you sell and are ready to buy it now.

Imagine if you knew the exact words in the right way and the right order so the people who are already searching for what you sell and are ready to buy it now will find you instantaneously?

Most businesses invest a lot of money to attract buyers online, yet not one in a hundred does a "magnetic keyword" analysis. We have an interview with an expert who knows how to reverse-engineer, find, and construct the perfect keyword phrase that will put you right in front of the people who are searching for what you sell and who are ready to buy it right now.

This interview will change your online marketing and help you be more successful. It can change how you language your value proposition. Finding your unique magnetic keyword phrase is the most important thing you must do first or next, before you spend another dime in online marketing. You can get access to this interview at www.thenewgameofselling.com/book.

PLAY 2: QUALIFY CUSTOMERS USING THE BUYING CYCLE

Play 2 in the *NEW* Game of Selling playbook is *qualify*. In other words, you want to know where your prospects are in the buying cycle. You meet them where they are.

The Buying Cycle

The buying cycle is about a person's state of readiness. Think about yourself right now. How committed are you to elevate your game of selling?

Are you ready, or are you just *getting* ready to take action?

There's a huge distinction between ready and getting ready. If you align with the buying cycle and meet people where they are, you'll never get frustrated again. You won't think you have a buyer when you really have a browser. You will know when a person is ready to buy.

There are three phases to the buying cycle:

- Phase I: Satisfied

- Phase II: Dissatisfied

- Phase III: Ready

Phase I in the buying cycle is *satisfied*. When you meet somebody who's satisfied with where they are and what they have, this is a *not* a buyer. She's not even a browser. If she is satisfied, she is disinterested.

When I got into insurance and financial planning, the training taught us to disturb people. They were telling us that satisfied people just don't know they should be dissatisfied. It was our job to disturb them into being dissatisfied. If we were really good, we could persuade them to see they have a big problem they need to solve right now. This was old-game selling.

How would you feel as a buyer if you are satisfied with your insurance, there is nothing you want to change, and I make up stories to disturb you? You'd kick me out the door if I try to create a nightmare scenario of what could happen to your family if you don't have life insurance. I destroy trust and extinguish any chance of having a business relationship with you in the future.

Why? Because I didn't align with where you were in the buying cycle.

Look at your pool of prospects right now. Those who are satisfied and disinterested, put back into your pipeline and educate them. Do not spend any time, energy, money, or resources on satisfied buyers.

If you have an unlimited supply of hungry fish who want your product or service right now, how much time would you spend with satisfied people? *None.*

Phase II in the buying cycle is *dissatisfied*. When people move from satisfied to dissatisfied, they become real buyers and start to get ready to purchase something new.

A Phase II person can be from 1 percent dissatisfied (mostly satisfied) to 99 percent dissatisfied (almost ready). She can be 211 degrees on a scale of 212, but not boiling yet.

Phase II is the Grand Canyon of lost opportunity, because a dissatisfied person is getting ready, yet we often mistake them for being ready. Here's a simple question you can ask every person to quickly identify this distinction:

"Are you ready, or are you getting ready?"

If she says "I'm ready," you want to activate her. You can present your solution to match what she is looking for. If she's still getting ready, and you launch into a pitch, presentation, or solution conversation, you break down alignment and jeopardize your relationship.

For people in Phase II, you help motivate them. Help them identify and define what will move them from getting ready to being ready.

In Play 4, we'll discuss in more detail what you do with a Phase II buyer.

Phase III in the buying cycle is ready. People who are ready are hungry fish. They are swimming around looking for the next meal.

The *NEW* Game of Selling is all about filling your pipeline with Phase III hungry fish.

Here's a valuable exercise to do right now:

• Categorize your prospects and potential buyers as Phase I, Phase II, or Phase III.

• Put the satisfied people back in your pipeline and educate them.

- Find out what will motivate dissatisfied people to move from getting ready to being ready. Determine if they are mildly dissatisfied or very dissatisfied. You want to know which buyers are one degree away from boiling.

- With ready buyers, activate them by matching your solution to their buying criteria.

You want to be in front of ready buyers all the time. When you have an unending stream of hungry fish ready to activate, you spend little time with Phase I and less time with Phase II buyers.

The RAMM Formula™

The RAMM formula is a model you can use to qualify a buyer and spend your time with hungry fish. Use the buying cycle to identify and categorize people as Phase I, II, or III buyers. Then apply the RAMM formula to qualify them in ten minutes or less.

You can also use The RAMM Formula to navigate and stay on course for any result you want.

RAMM is an acronym for this four-step formula:

- Result

- Action

- Measure

- Modify

R = Result. What's your destination, your point B? Where are you going? The first thing I want to know about my customers is the result they are looking for. If I don't know where they're going, how can I help them get there? The same is true for you in the business game. Step one in the RAMM formula is to identify your desired result. What's your destination?

A = Action. What action are you taking right now? Everybody tells you to take action. Some people are just stuck in inertia. A body at rest stays at rest, and a body in motion continues in motion. If your customer is stuck in inertia, how can you help them get into motion?

If you are stuck in the business game, remember that *NEW* Game players take imperfect action. I created this mantra to combat my perfectionism and get me into motion:

"Take imperfect action, because imperfect action beats perfect inaction."

M = Measure. Are you on or off course for point B? If your actions are moving you farther away from your result and you don't measure, you won't know if you're on or off course. You'll look up one day and find you're 20 degrees off course. I ask the simple question,

"Are you on or off course for your result or to get where you're going?"

In some cases, people I meet are so far off course it's almost impossible to turn the jumbo jet around in enough time to safely get them where they want to go.

Having to take emergency procedures or make radical course corrections is not a comfortable or anxiety-free way to transport people from point A to point B.

Measure both quality and quantity. Measure quality by how much you enjoy your livelihood, serve people, and play for the love of the game. Measure quantity in your sales and income numbers.

Measure to see if you're on or off course.

M = Modify. What change or correction will you make? This is the critical step that tells you where a person is in the buying cycle. If you go through the RAMM formula—Result, Action, Measure, Modify— and you discover a person is not ready to modify, change, revise, or course correct, then you know she's not ready to change. Ask your customer the "Modify" question, and you'll know whether she is ready or just getting ready:

What are you willing to shift, revise, alter, adjust, or change—and when?

If she's not ready to shift, revise, alter, adjust, or change, she's not ready to buy. You cannot activate her unless and until she is really ready. You want her to say "I'm ready," or "This is when I'm going to be ready"—tomorrow, next week, or next month.

The old game was about persuading buyers to be ready.

The *NEW* Game is about finding ready buyers and being the only game in town when they are getting ready.

The RAMM formula will help you to qualify people fast and gracefully. You're doing a great service by helping a person see the four-step "flight plan" she must follow to get what she wants.

(BONUS: Download RAMM Formula worksheets at www.thenewgameofselling.com/book.)

A powerful formula for qualifying people, it's just as valuable as your personal navigational tool to keep you on course for your destination.

Use RAMM to qualify people, identify where they are in the buying cycle, and meet them where they are. Determine if they are ready to make a change, and if so, when. This tells you which phase of the buying cycle they're in.

Now, it's time to cash in. Conversion turns marketing expense into sales revenue.

PLAY 3: CONVERT BROWSERS INTO BUYERS WITH THREE MAGIC WORDS

Conversion is the part of selling that creates the most stress and causes the biggest challenge. When I first started selling, I had a hard time converting browsers to buyers—or closing the sale.

Old-game sales training taught 24 ways to close the sale. No part of the buying or selling process creates more fear, dread, and anxiety than conversion.

In the *NEW* Game of Selling, we don't close sales.

We gain commitment.

The two conversion models you're about to learn will be worth hundreds, maybe thousands of times your investment in this book. They're going to be self-evident once you see them. They have transformed businesses and contributed to billions of dollars in new sales for thousands of companies from Fortune 500s to small businesses to the self-employed.

Three Magic Words

The first model I call "three magic words." This model can affect every relationship you have. You can use it to advance a relationship in any area of your business and life.

The three magic words are *alignment, agreement,* and *commitment.*

The visual I use is three green lights to represent the three magic words. Picture this. You're with a potential buyer, walking arm in arm together to her destination. To reach the "Promised Land," you need to pass the three green lights of alignment, agreement, and commitment.

Alignment

Alignment is trust. It's credibility, confidence, and connection. Alignment means we're on the same page.

Alignment asks:

- Why are we here?

- What is our outcome?

- What's the purpose of this conversation?

You can get alignment in advance by giving your customers useful insights, valuable content, and establishing trust before you walk through the door. With a referral or third-party endorsement, you walk in with a higher degree of alignment than if you have to build alignment with somebody you've never met before.

Building alignment with a person you've just met takes time, trust, and conversation. Many relationships break down in this stage because buyer and seller are not aligned. Usually it's because the seller is racing ahead. You won't get to the second green light if the alignment light doesn't turn green.

Get alignment before you move to the next green light.

Agreement

Agreement asks:

- What do you want?

- Why do you want it?

- How do you want it?

- When do you want it?

I recommend you get everything on the table that your buyer wants, and then ask him to agree to it. We are agreeing on what you want, why, how, and when.

When you know what they want, why, the way they want it, and when they want it, you now have agreement. You can pass the second green light.

Imagine what happens if you blow past alignment and you don't have trust? You're not on the same page. You have different agendas. All of a sudden, you ask her to reveal what she wants, how, why, and when. She's hesitant because she doesn't feel the alignment of credibility, confidence and connection. She won't walk through the red light of alignment so you can get to agreement. No alignment, no agreement.

What if you're walking through the first light, and all of a sudden the light turns red? If you try to push someone to cross the street at a red light, she'll say, "No, I've got to wait until the light turns green." If you try to get agreement before you have alignment, the light turns red. At best, you're out of alignment. At worst, the game can be over right here.

You may have thought you had alignment, but you never got it or you lost it. You don't have the green light to go to agreement. If people share anything with you at all about what they want, why, how, and when, it will be filtered through a lack of trust.

Without credibility, confidence, and connection, you and your buyer feel like you're not on the same page—because you're not.

Look at all your relationships. With those you have alignment, move to agreement. If you don't have alignment or you're not sure, go back and start over again. Get alignment. Then get agreement.

Once you have agreement on what they want, why they want it, how they want it, and when they want it, the third magic word is *commitment*.

Commitment

Commitment asks, "What are you ready, committed, and willing to do next?"

Think about this carefully. It's a game changer.

If you do all the work—if you do proposals, illustrations, and give them all kinds of information—but they do nothing in return, you are stalled. Momentum and motion stop. You're on hold and in limbo. If your buyer has no commitment to act and is not willing to do something, she can't get what she wants.

Until *she* is ready, committed and willing, *you* will never make that sale.

Do you believe that if you do enough work, people will appreciate your work and buy just because you did the work? I've done "the work" more times than I can count. I figured if I do extra work, maybe she'll appreciate that and be more likely to make a commitment.

That's not how commitment works. Commitment answers the question,

"What is the buyer willing to do?"

Commitment transforms your entire conversion strategy.

You can look at every relationship you have in limbo or in process and apply these three magic words to it. You can look at the people who have not made a commitment to work with you, or who were not willing to do something, and revisit them. It's likely you don't have alignment or agreement—possibly both.

Or, you may have alignment and agreement, but he's not ready to make a commitment. Until he is committed, he won't do something. Once he's committed, you have a ready buyer.

Take your entire population of people, including your clients, and reexamine, redefine, and reengage with them. Talk about the three magic words.

1. Are we in alignment?

2. Do we have agreement on what you want, why, how, and when?

3. Are you committed to do something now to get what you want?

Here's how you know if you've advanced the relationship:

The buyer says yes to all three magic words and commits to take a specific action.

If there's no commitment to do something now or next, the relationship is stalled right now in the commitment phase. That doesn't mean it's stalled forever.

In the next conversion model, we'll show you how to get things moving again.

My guess is you have a host of opportunities to revisit prospects and past buyers, get alignment, and find agreement. You can ask people what they are willing to commit to do now to get what they want. Just by going through this process, you'll advance relationships and make some sales. For those people who are stalled right now, you'll discover exactly where they're stalled and get the game going again.

You're not guessing, and you are not confused any more. You know exactly what to do to advance the relationship with every person in every situation.

Is this cool, or what? I've used the three magic words thousands of times, and I've trained tens of thousands of professionals to use this every day. You can use these three magic words with your family, friends, and personal relationships to get alignment, agreement, and commitment.

The game is to advance together through three green lights. If any of the lights turn red, you STOP, and go back to the preceding light. If you're not sure where you are, then start all over.

Get alignment. Get agreement. Get commitment.

The three magic words will change everything in your business and personal relationships.

Cost/Value Formula

Can you move a person from getting ready to being ready? What can you say or do to gain commitment?

This conversion model enables you to get buy-in by helping people make a good decision. I call it the *cost/value formula*. You assist a buyer to determine the cost of the problem and the value of the solution.

Every buying decision is triggered by emotion and then justified with logic. When people are in Phase II of the buying cycle, they're still getting ready. They reach a point when they need to see and compare the cost of the problem with the value of a solution.

This evaluation is often not conscious, but you want to make it conscious. For people who are not yet ready, you help them discover and have them express what will make them ready.

You help them evaluate the cost of the problem and compare it to the value of the solution.

You start by asking them, "What are the consequences, ramifications, and implications if you maintain the status quo and do nothing?"

This is your role as a valued professional, the trusted voice of choice who acts as the *consigliere* and advisor. You guide people in evaluating the consequences, ramifications, and implications of their problem, and compare them to the value, payoff, and reward of a solution.

You help them see clearly the financial, emotional, psychological, operational, and spiritual cost of keeping the problem, and the value of solving it. You give control to the buyer to decide if it makes more sense to stay in status quo, or make a change.

Become skilled at guiding people to see the difference between the cost of their problem and the value of a solution. Improve your ability to draw out consequences, ramifications, and implications of what will happen if they do nothing. Get agreement on the value of the solution. Ask them to tell you the payoff, reward, and benefit of acting or changing.

You will be seen in a whole new and completely different light. This is a questioning model. You're not telling them the cost, consequences, ramifications, or implications. You're not telling them what the payoff, reward, or value is. You are empowering and encouraging people to feel, think, and evaluate for themselves.

You collaborate with them to come up with answers to cost and value. In the end, you ask,

"What makes more sense and is in your best interest: to do nothing or do something?"

Do you keep your problem, or are you ready to change right now?

Apply the cost/value model to every person who has not yet made a commitment.

PLAY 4: KEEP CUSTOMERS COMING BACK FOR LIFE ... ASK FIVE QUESTIONS OF SERVICE

How do you keep customers coming back for life and buying more?

Ask the Five Questions of Service™. These five questions have created hundreds of millions of dollars in new revenue through additional sales, testimonials, endorsements, and referrals.

When you look at our success stories page (www.thenewgameofselling.com/successstories), you'll see powerful testimonials and ringing endorsements from clients, colleagues, and experts. How did I get them?

I asked the Five Questions of Service. These "5" questions form the first part of the 5-4-3-2-1 MEGA-Referrals™ system. (You get MEGA-Referrals training FREE, included in the book buyer's special "Incredible" deal. Find details at www.thenewgameofselling.com/book.)

We encourage all of our clients to use the Five Questions of Service or a variation of the theme. If you ask these five questions, you will keep more customers, get more referrals, elicit powerful testimonials, and receive ringing endorsements. You'll increase your profit and boost your customer value.

Service Question 1: Why Did You Buy from Me/Us?

We introduced Service Question 1 earlier. It is the most important question of all. Ask this question of everyone who buys from you. Ask it of the people who left, disappeared, or stopped buying. This one question gives you an enormous amount of vital and valuable insight.

You can also ask this question of customers from other vendors or your competition: "Why did you buy from that person or company?"

You will know more about what you do in your customers' words. This question helps you discover and articulate your USA—your Unique Service Advantage. Your USA is what makes you, your product, your service, or your approach unique, distinct, and most valuable to your customers.

Go back to your 10, 20, 50, or 100 best clients and ask them why they bought from you. Get them to talk about their experience. Encourage them to elaborate and, most of all, ask them to be as specific as possible.

When you really know why people buy, you can use these four powerful words with new buyers:

"Our customers tell us…."

What do your customers tell you? You won't know until you ask them, "Why did you buy from me?"

So…why did you buy this book?

(You can answer all 5 Questions of Service for this book at www.thenewgameofselling.com/book)

Service Question 2: How Do You Feel about the Work We've Done?

You want to know how she feels more than what she thinks. Remember, all buying decisions are triggered by emotion and supported with logic and reason. You want to discover the emotional connection that caused her to buy. This "E-Link" or emotional link is the strongest feeling at the heart of the buying decision.

Ask people to expand and elaborate on how they feel. Write down the responses to this question. They supply you with powerful emotional language to support your USA and share with new buyers.

How do you feel about the value you're getting from reading this book?

Service Question 3: What Are You Happiest With and Most Satisfied About?

Here you want people to share their qualitative emotional experience and quantitative results. What they are happiest with and most satisfied about tells you how well you're playing the game. Their answers enable you to expand on the phrase, "Our customers tell us…."

What are your customers telling you they are happiest with and most satisfied about?

What are you happiest with and most satisfied about this book?

Service Question 4: If You Had to Do It Over, What Would You Change or Do Differently?

This is the critical pivot question that gets you more business right now from people who are ready to buy again. It also reveals the gap between what they bought and where they are now. It lets you know where your customer is in a new buying cycle.

Consultants use zero-based thinking. Service Question 4 is a zero-based question that asks:

"If you knew then what you know now, what would you change or do differently?"

I have an example from my financial planning days. I asked a client this question, and I was afraid he was going to say, "I would have bought less life insurance."

It turns out he said, "If I had to do it differently, or go back and do it all over again, I would have bought $500,000 instead of $250,000 worth of life insurance."

He revealed he was off course from his point A to point B. I made that extra $250,000 sale simply by asking him what he would change or do differently if he could do it all over again. No pushing, shoving, hard selling, or closing technique.

By asking this one question, I served my client and doubled my commission.

How many of your customers would buy again *right now* if you simply asked them Service Question 4?

This question is going to change your business and your life. You'll be blown away at how easy it is to make another sale. If you have never asked this question of your prospects, you'll be equally surprised at the number of people who would love a "do-over" to go back and start again.

Think about a person who's buying from someone else who could be your customer. Call him and ask what he would change or do differently if he could do it all over again. He just might tell you everything to get his business, because you know what his vendor or supplier doesn't know. Because you're focused on helping to transport that person who has just said he is now off course, you've positioned yourself as a trusted voice of choice. There's a strong chance you can attract and convert that person into a new customer.

Ask at least one customer every day, "What would you change or do differently?"

What would you change or do differently about reading this book?

Service Question 5: How Can I Better Serve You Now, and in the Future?

Do you ask this question of all of your customers? Do you ask it at all? This question enhances client retention, tells you what's next, and often results in new sales. The game is not about perfection. It's about progress and improvement. Start asking everyone (buyers, prospects, other people's customers):

"How can I better serve you now, and in the future?"

You will transform relationships and create new customers right now. When people tell you how they want to be better served, there's a strong possibility they're dissatisfied, or ready to buy something new or something else. By asking the question, you're in the game.

The Five Questions of Service provide a great opportunity to secure referrals, testimonials, and endorsements. Through their answers, your clients tell you how well you've done and the advantages of working with you. Also, you can ask customers with confidence and enthusiasm to introduce you to other people who want to be served in the same way.

The Five Questions of Service retain your customers in the game for the long haul and keep them coming back for more.

Play 5: Multiply Customer Value through Upsell, Backend, and Cross-Sell

There are many ways to multiply customer value. These three are the easiest and most effective, with many subcategories within:

1. Upsell

2. Backend

3. Cross-sell

Upsell

Every additional sale to a customer is less expensive and creates more bottom-line profit for you. You can increase customer profitability from 300 percent to 900 percent with a simple add-on or upsell at the point of purchase. The classic (and worn out) example is McDonald's "Do you want fries with your burger?"

When a person buys, ask what else they want and/or offer an upsell.

You can bump, bundle, bargain, and borrow customers:

• Bump up to a bigger or better package.

• Bundle another product or service together.

• Bargain by offering a whole lot more for a whole lot less if they buy now.

- Borrow customers by partnering and/or joint venturing with other businesses whose audiences are your buyers and that want a new source of revenue and profit.

These all lead to backend selling.

Backend

The answer to the question, "How can I serve you better now or in the future?" often reveals your customer's next purchase. Ask people straight out:

"What would you like to do next? Then what will you do after that?"

You're charting the future by asking people about their next destination. Remember, you're in the transportation business. If you're helping to transport me from point A to point B, what else do I need on that journey to get there faster and easier with less stress and tension?

That next step can be an add-on or complementary buy at the point of purchase, or a backend sale for your next conversation or appointment. That's why you don't "close the sale" and run away. You want to meet again and discuss their next step. Get comfortable asking people,

"What will you do next? What comes after that?"

When you know where people are going and what they need to get there, every additional purchase is a vehicle to help transport them from where they are to where they want to be.

The more you know about what they want to do next and after that, the easier it is for you to give them what you have or might be able to get from a third party.

That leads us to cross-selling.

Cross-Sell

If you look at your entire population of prospects, what percentage has not bought from you?

If your buyer doesn't want your product or service, why not consider cross-selling somebody else's product or service? This means joint venturing and/or partnering with other suppliers who can offer complimentary products and services.

Create and/or expand your network of joint ventures or partners who can cross-sell your product or service to other people, or who can sell their product or service to your customers. What kinds of other products and services do you or could you offer to people who don't buy from you?

A good number of your prospects and customers might be candidates for something else, but you've never invited them in. You've never asked them what else, what next, and what after that?

The Five Questions of Service can also transform how your customers see you.

You will pick up extra business just by asking the questions.

Upselling, backend, and cross-selling open up big opportunities for you to capitalize with little or no additional cost or expense. Do you think that by offering something new or different to your customers, they might leave? Some might. Most will be grateful to know you're looking out for their best interest. They take your recommendation because you are the most trusted voice of choice.

The truth is the more people buy from you, even if it's somebody else's product, the more likely they are to stay loyal to you as a lifetime customer. Serve, deliver, and serve some more.

You now have five plays to attract, qualify, convert, keep, and multiply customers.

That's how you play and win the *NEW* Game of Selling.

WHAT NOW, WHAT NEXT? HOW TO WIN THE *NEW* GAME OF SELLING

Here are the next steps you can take right now.

1. For your FREE bonus material visit www.thenewgameofselling.com/book Here is your personal code for this book only to log in and unlock your access: **yR68kUzH.**

Free video training for buying this book. Apply this free training and watch your game change right before your eyes.

The Billion-Dollar Playbook. The Billion-Dollar Playbook contains the most successful plays that win the *NEW* Game of Selling.

Supplemental material, live training, and exclusive special offers and discounts.

2. Get *The NEW Game of Selling* training book buyer's exclusive "Insider" special

As a book buyer, you receive our very best "Incredible" deal. Get instant access to the entire training, action guides, worksheets, supplemental materials, word for word transcript, PLUS bonus Players Club membership with dozens of coaching sessions and LIVE monthly coaching. Get the secret link to the "Incredible" deal at the book bonus page here www.thenewgameofselling.com/book.

3. Bring the *NEW* Game of Selling to your company.

I encourage you to bring *The NEW Game of Selling* training into your company; you really can't lose. At the book bonus site, you'll see a way to contact us to become one of our "Preferred Partners"—go to www.thenewgameofselling.com/book and use your access code: **yR68kUzH**.

Winston Churchill once said:

We stumble over the truth from time to time, but most of us pick ourselves up and hurry off as if nothing ever happened.

We covered a lot of truth in this playbook. The *NEW* Game plays will change your sales game.

Whichever phase of your business you can best leverage right now, take imperfect action and apply what you've learned. Make a difference for yourself and your customers. Things will never be the same when you play the *NEW* Game. You will attract, qualify, convert, keep, and multiply customers *now*!

You're a player.

You *can* change the game.

I'll meet you on the field again very soon.

ABOUT THE AUTHOR

Mitchell Axelrod is founder of Axelrod & Associates, a business consulting firm, and The *NEW* Game Media, a publisher of business and life skills books, training, workshops and professional learning materials. Mitch has presented more than 3,500 seminars, workshops, keynotes, webinars, teleconferences and clinics to more than a million people on entrepreurship, business, sales, marketing, life skills and playing the new game.

Creator of The *NEW* Game™ series, Mitch is the author of The *NEW* Game of Business™, The *NEW* Game of IP™ (Intellectual Property) and the Amazon #1 bestseller, The *NEW* Game of Selling™. He has reached millions of people through radio, television, audio and video. His articles, special reports, newsletters, white papers and training programs are used in 35 countries. An intellectual property specialist, he licenses IP and pioneered the "rent your content" strategy.

Mitch's strategies have generated billions of

dollars of additional revenue for thousands of companies from Fortune 500's IBM, AT&T, MetLife, Citibank, Pfizer, and Prudential to small, medium and home based businesses. He has shared the stage with the world's leading speakers, experts and authors including Jack Canfield, Denis Waitley, Barbara Corcoran, Brian Tracy, Mark Victor Hansen, John Assaraf, Mari Smith, Jay Abraham, Michael Gerber, Les Brown, Loral Langemeier, T. Harv Eker, Dan Kennedy, and dozens more.

Mitch plays for the love of the game. Known as the CEO - Chief Encouragement Officer - he inspires us to elevate our play and up our game. His collaboration transforms companies, culture and profitability. His peers call him the "Mentor the the Masters" for his advice, counsel and commitment to their highest and best interests. Mitch's proudest accomplishment is the 10 years he invested as a stay at home, single Dad.

Mitch is available to speak, train and consult. Visit his personal website at:

www.mitchaxelrod.com